CHORD

CHORD

POEMS

RICK BAROT

Sarabande  Books

LOUISVILLE, KENTUCKY

Managing Editor
Sarabande Books, Inc.
2234 Dundee Road, Suite 200
Louisville, KY 40205

Library of Congress Cataloging-in-Publication Data

Barot, Rick, 1969–
[Poems. Selections]
Chord / Rick Barot. — First edition.
    pages ; cm.
ISBN 978-1-941411-03-2 (softcover : acid-free paper)
I. Title.
PS3602.A835A6 2015
811'.6—dc23

                         2014032732

Cover image: "Landscape #7" by Vanessa Marsh. Pigment print from
Photogram Negative. Image copyright © 2014 Vanessa Marsh.

Design by Kirkby Gann Tittle.

Manufactured in Canada.

This book is printed on acid-free paper.

Sarabande Books is a nonprofit literary organization.

This project is supported in part by an award from the National Endowment
for the Arts.

The Kentucky Arts Council, the state arts agency, supports Sarabande Books
with state tax dollars and federal funding from the National Endowment for
the Arts.

to my comrades—
Michael Dumanis, Rigoberto González,
Salvatore Scibona, C. Dale Young

CONTENTS

Acknowledgments / *ix*

I

Tarp / 3
On Gardens / 5
Looking at the Romans / 7
Black Canvas / 8
The Wooden Overcoat / 10
The Documents of Spring / 11
Child Holding Potato / 14
Some Roses & Their Phantoms / 15
The Poem is a Letter Opener / 19

II

Brown Refrigerator / 23
Daguerreotypes / 25
Ode: 1975 / 28
Particle and Wave / 30
Virgin of Guadalupe / 32
Ode: 1986 / 34
Question Arising While Listening
to a Lecture on the Nature of Metaphor / 36
Tacoma Lyric / 38
Chord / 40

III

Inventory / 47
Syntax / 48
Whitman, 1841 / 50

Exegesis in Wartime / 52
Election Song / 55
The Man with the Crew-Cut / 57
Coast Starlight / 58
Triptych / 59
After Darwish / 64

The Author / 67

ACKNOWLEDGMENTS

I am grateful to the editors and staff of the following publications, where the poems in this book first appeared: *American Poetry Review, The Asian American Literary Review, The Carolina Quarterly, Cerise Press, Diode, Gulf Coast, The Kenyon Review, Memorious, The New Republic, Ploughshares, Poetry, Poetry Northwest, The Threepenny Review, Tin House, Tongue, TriQuarterly, Waxwing, West Branch Wired, ZYZZYVA.*

"Child Holding Potato" was reprinted in *The Best American Poetry 2012* (Scribner). "Ode: 1975," "Ode: 1986," and "Particle and Wave" were reprinted in *Field of Mirrors: An Anthology of Philippine American Writers* (PAWA Press). "Election Song" was reprinted in *In Tahoma's Shadow* (Exquisite Disarray Publishing). "Whidbey Island" was reprinted in *Alive at the Center* (Ooligan Press). "After Darwish," "Inventory," and "The Poem Is a Letter Opener" were reprinted in *The Rag-Picker's Guide to Poetry: Poems, Poets, Process* (University of Michigan Press). "Looking at the Romans" was reprinted on *Poetry Daily*. "Brown Refrigerator" was reprinted on *Verse Daily*.

I am indebted to the Artist Trust of Washington, the Civitella Ranieri Foundation, the MacDowell Colony, and Pacific Lutheran University. Last but nowhere least, my thanks to the good people of Sarabande Books for their continuing support of my work.

TARP

I have seen the black sheets laid out like carpets
under the trees, catching the rain

of olives as they fell. Also the cerulean brightness
of the one covering the bad roof

of a neighbor's shed, the color the only color
inside the winter's weeks. Another one

took the shape of the pile of bricks underneath.
Another flew off the back of a truck,

black as a piano if a piano could rise into the air.
I have seen the ones under bridges,

the forms they make of sleep. I could go on
this way until the end of the page, even though

what I have in my mind isn't the thing
itself, but the category of belief that sees the thing

as a shelter for what is beneath it.
There is no shelter. You cannot put a tarp over

a wave. You cannot put a tarp
over a war. You cannot put a tarp over the broken

oil well miles under the ocean.
There is no tarp for that raging figure in the mind

that sits in a corner and shreds receipts
and newspapers. There is no tarp for dread,

whose only recourse is language
so approximate it hardly means what it means:

He is not here. She is sick. She cannot remember
her name. He is old. He is ashamed.

ON GARDENS

When I read about the garden
designed to bloom only white flowers,
I think about the Spanish friar who saw one
of my grandmothers, two hundred years
removed, and fucked her. If you look
at the word *colony* far enough, you see it
travelling back to the Latin
of *inhabit*, *till*, and *cultivate*. Words

that would have meant something
to the friar, walking among the village girls
as though in a field of flowers, knowing
that fucking was one way of having
a foreign policy. As I write this, there's snow
falling, which means that every
angry thought is as short-lived as a match.
The night is its own white garden:

snow on the fence, snow on the tree
stump, snow on the azalea bushes,
their leaves hanging down like green
bats from the branches. I know it's not fair
to see qualities of injustice in the aesthetics
of a garden, but somewhere between
what the eye sees and what the mind thinks
is the world, landscapes mangled

into sentences, one color read into rage.
When the neighbors complained
the roots of our cypress were buckling
their lot, my landlord cut the tree down.
I didn't know a living thing three stories high

could be so silent, until it was gone.
Suddenly that sky. Suddenly all the light
in the windows, as though every sheet

of glass was having a migraine.
When I think about that grandmother
whose name I don't even know, I think of
what it would mean to make a garden
that blooms black: peonies and gladiolas
of deepest purple, tulips like ravens.
Or a garden that doesn't bloom at all: rocks
placed on a plane of raked gravel,

the stray leaves cleared away every hour.
If you look at the word *garden*
deep enough, you see it blossoming
in an enclosure meant to keep out history
and disorder. Like the neighbors wanting
to keep the cypress out. Like the monks
arranging the stones into an image
of serenity. When the snow stops, I walk to see

the quiet that has colonized everything.
The main street is asleep, except for the bus
that goes by, bright as a cruise ship.
There are sheet-cakes of snow on top
of cars. In front of houses, each lawn
is as clean as paper, except where the first cat
or raccoon has walked across, each track
like a barbed-wire sash on a white gown.

LOOKING AT THE ROMANS

in the museum, the heavy marble busts
on their white plinths, I recognize one likeness
as my uncle, the retired accountant
whose mind, like a conquered country, is turning
into desert, into the dust of forgotten things.
The white head of an old man, big as a god,
its short curled hair still rich
as matted grass, is my grandmother,
a Roman on her deathbed, surrounded
by a citizenry of keening, her breaths rising out
of the dark of a well, the orange medicine bottles
massed like an emergency on the table.
The delicate face of the serious young man
is another uncle, the one who lost
his friends when a plane hit their aircraft carrier,
the one who dropped pomegranate fires
on the scattering villagers, on the small
brown people who looked like him.
One bust is of a noblewoman, the pleats
of her toga articulated into silky marble folds,
her hair carved into singular strands:
she is the aunt who sends all her money home,
to lazy sons and dying neighbors.
Another marble woman is my other aunt,
the one who grows guavas and persimmons,
the one who dries salted fish on her garage roof,
as though she were still mourning
the provinces. Here is the cousin who is a priest.
Here is the cousin who sells drugs.
Here is the other grandmother, her heart still
skilled at keeping time. Here is my mother
in the clear pale face of a Roman's wife,
a figure moving softly, among flowers and slaves.

BLACK CANVAS

The painter believes he can see better
by not seeing at all, so in the dark of his studio
he paints the dark. The canvases look like
oil slicks or nights without stars. In faintly brushed
arcs, white appears on the rough black,
as though to show where the light continues

to stay in the room: a glint on a ficus-leaf's edge,
a smudge on a mirror. Art in its intention
wants to be in the condition of poetry,
but most art is in the condition of prose.
This is not a slander to prose. Prose is what happens
when we watched a backyard rat die

during a hot Los Angeles afternoon, while
inside, a party ignited for an uncle turning
seventy-five. The rat had scurried across the yard,
stopped midway, and didn't move again
except to drag towards a brick planter,
where it finally stopped, its face to the brick side,

its back pumping irregularly. At first
the children toyed with it, until the dark import
became clear: dying was the afternoon
lesson. There were two tables of food, three
birthday cakes, a whole suckling pig, an apple shiny
in its mouth, its legs like a racehorse

on the run, all feet off the ground.
When my friend and I saw the black paintings
in the gallery, he said that a trip
to Home Depot and he could make what

was in front of us. The point made me realize that
what's visible isn't always superior

to what can't be seen, like ideas proven only
by poor means, as though the invisible
were a ventriloquist saying something important
with his mouth shut. The dying of the rat required
the rat to be there, its own illustration.
The dying of the uncle required that he be

at his birthday party, though certain cells, like ravens
in a winter landscape, winged through
his body, a slander to the man blowing out
seventy-five candles on three birthday cakes.
Because one condition of art is that it tries too hard,
in his studio the painter mixes twigs and sand

into the tub of black paint, a substance
active as tar, spread on the canvas like a road.
For the painter, there are stones, objects turned
now to stone, all kinds of ruin to plant
into the canvas. The things that don't need any more
light. Only more dark growing in the dark.

THE WOODEN OVERCOAT

It turns out there's a difference between a *detail*
and an *image*. If a dandelion on the sidewalk is
mere detail, the dandelion inked on a friend's bicep
is an image because it moves when her body does,
even when a shirt covers up the little black sun

on a thin stalk. The same way that the barcode
on the back of another friend's neck is just a detail,
until you hear that the row of numbers underneath
are the numbers his grandfather got on his arm
in a camp in Poland. Then it's an image, something

activated in the reader's senses beyond mere fact.
I know the difference doesn't matter, except in poetry,
where a coffin is just another coffin until someone
at a funeral calls it a *wooden overcoat*, an image
so heavy and warm at the same time that you forget

it's about death. At my uncle's funeral, the coffin
was so beautiful it was like the chandelier lighting
the room where treaties are signed. It made me think
of how loved he was. It made me think of Shoshone
funerals, where everything the dead person owned

was put into a bonfire, even the horse. In that last
sentence, is the horse a detail or an image? I don't
really know. In my mind, a horse is never anywhere
near a fire, and a detail is as luminous as an image:
the trumpet-vine, the fence, the clothes, the fire.

THE DOCUMENTS OF SPRING

I was told once that having so many birds
in my poetry meant that it was
all sentimental, that birds weren't
the real world, but a way of always dodging
the important questions.
I believed this for about a week, until

looking one afternoon
out my kitchen window, thinking hard
about one of those big questions, I saw a small
brown bird on top of the fence
fly up briefly to let a scampering squirrel
pass by, then fly back down again,

to the exact spot where it had been.
The bird was the color of dark sand, with
black markings dotted on it.
It was food for the eye's moment, the way,
on another moment, it would be actual
food, like the remaining thing left

on my doormat by the neighborhood cat
one morning, a full-spread wing
ripped from a body. The cat meant it
as offering, because I had been feeding him
when he came by, when he made a circuit
in my house in the afternoon hours:

sleeping on the trapezoid of sunshine
on the linoleum kitchen floor, on the left side
of the sofa, under the bed, and, once,
drinking in the toilet in a truly

agile crouch, a position that didn't startle
when I walked past. But the wing:

it was a few inches across, smoke-colored
like the cat, with the torn edge bloody
and bony, a screaming meat of face
in a painting by Francis Bacon. Later, still
lying there on the front porch,
ants had started in on it, a roiling of desire.

The big question I had in mind
was about the hate that could pass between
two people yet not destroy them completely,
on the spot, that very instant
one is sending the bat-black words
to the other, and then hanging up the phone,

fast. It was going to be our mother's
sixtieth birthday, and here we were,
my sister and I, arguing about what to do
about it. The argument was
about everything: the time she smashed a toy
airplane to my forehead, the time she

sliced my cheek with a cracker, the time
I pushed her down a rubble heap
we were playing on, opening up her leg
on a stub of rebar. The bird on
the fence was like a song to our malfeasances,
like water poured over our malfeasances,

a lifetime of such things. This was one thing
the bird could mean, one thing I could
force from it. Because mostly it was just
what it was, and nothing else.
It was not song, not love, not forgiveness.
It was not a nagging to call back, which I didn't,

and haven't. In my town this time of year,
in every yard of every house,
the azaleas bloom, in a display that even
the dullest-eyed of us cannot miss:
purples and reds, explosive as tango gestures,
powder pinks, like the teacups

of little girls, and bright whites, the blank
documents of spring. I drive around repeating
to myself: *azaleas and so on, azaleas
and so on*. Thinking that no good has ever come
of any word I've made, spoken, or borrowed:
azaleas and so on, azaleas and so on.

CHILD HOLDING POTATO

When my sister got her diagnosis,
I bought an airplane ticket

but to another city, where I stared
at paintings that seemed victorious

in their relation to time.
The beech from two hundred years ago,

its trunk a palette of mud
and gilt. The man with olive-black

gloves, the sky behind him
a glacier of blue light. In their calm

landscapes, the saints. Still dripping
the garden's dew, the bouquets.

Holding the rough gold orb
of a potato, the Child cradled

by the glowing Madonna. Then,
the paintings I looked at the longest:

the bowls of plums and peaches,
the lemons, the pomegranates

like red earths. In my mouth,
the raw starch. In my mouth, the dirt.

SOME ROSES & THEIR PHANTOMS

—for, and after, Brian Teare

There is still life and then
      there is this painting: everything
      in it is so much in flux it is against

the idea of still, the room made to seem
      fleeing from what it contains:
      the tilted tablescape of gray

roses, the jaggedly wrinkled
      tablecloth and the various grays
      of the roses, the fullness of it all

so that the mind and eye disagree
      a little: the eye seeing a good
      flood, which the mind reads

as darkness imagined, an interior depleted
      to a painting of roses that have lost
      what they usually mean:

gone, the sweetness of love tokened
      by the bloom's usual red, which is
      cousin to the red pomegranate

that means resurrection, cousin to the grapes
      that will be the wine that will be
      the blood, cousin to the white

jasmine that also means love's sweetness,
      sprigs of them in the old
      paintings like an incidental

knowledge, though it is always that
        offhand specificity I look for, my eye
        for example now walking past

the sill and glass to the syllables of yellow
        leaves, first among the late
        green outside: "As you *see* so at length

you will *say*," one philosopher says,
        which must mean what, exactly,
        to the one looking at the walls

tilting inward in the painting, the table's two
        legs short, two long, the roses
        gray as a collapsed building,

the floor angled up to meet
        the ceiling's face: roses are not
        always red, violets are not

always blue, you are there and I am
        in the woods, the shifting of leaves
        at times like a glimpse

at a comical stranger, then quiet
        again, the eye taken back inside:
        the Fuji of spilled sugar

on the counter, beside it the moon of spoon,
        the boiling eggs knocking
        morse into each other:

one poet saying, "Patience is
      the spectre of want," another
      poet saying, "And I not a rib of his,"

both saying the same thing about longing:
      days ago, after an argument,
      we stared over the pier

to the moss-green water: fish, thin
      as pens, rose to the surface, then
      jerked away to some

other depth; for a moment inhabiting
      the outlined shapes
      our shadows made on the water,

they were like thoughts in our bodies,
      actively quiet, moving
      but not touching each other,

different but coming from the same being,
      the same dark clear
      element: another poet

saying, "What is it then between us?
      What is the count /
      of the scores / or hundreds of years

between us?": which is a question
      I might ask myself, thinking that
      the last time I was in these

woods, the towers had not fallen, though
      they would days later,
      the smoke-clouds like gray

roses, the smoke like the smoke-like
      fish in water: everything in flux,
      as though against the very

idea of seeing: the buildings and the roses
      like the difference
      between what the mind thinks—

my translation stops working, though
      the heart keeps challenging
      my ability to make any mark,

and in that search for feeling is an honest
      danger, a temptation
      to fulfill feeling in a wrong way—

and what the eye sees: in an old painting,
      the saint pulls a thorn from
      a lion's paw; in the woods, lichen

like cobwebs on a rock; in the painting,
      the roses the color
      of scalding water from the tap.

THE POEM IS A LETTER OPENER

and it is the letter that is answered
or not answered, held first by the uncle
who sorted it on his graveyard shift
in the postal service warehouse,
after which it became the postman
going from box to box, each box
a particular face like a dog's, the dog
that is also a poem, its eyes dark
like the water in a well, its fur smelling
like grass that is also a poem, green
and exclamatory in spring, later
turning the color of rubber-bands,
which are also poems, holding
together the pencils, the tip-money,
the small stone in the sling-shot right
before it takes flight, the stone that
looks like a tiny skull, granite like death,
a piece of the night left in the middle
of the day, which is also a poem,
starting with its whisper campaign
of morning light, the light touching
the clean sidewalk, the light touching
the sign in the window that says
"No Crying Allowed In Tattoo Shop,"
the sign itself a poem, like the dusk
arriving around us, a cowl around us,
to the sick uncle, to the thieving uncle,
to the uncle who sleeps in the day,
his sleep careful as a tea ceremony
or a poem, a poem that is old and full
of days, a poem like an old china
plate that is the color of time, the dusk

having its supper of fog and people
walking through the fog, the fallen
leaves in the parks like strewn credit
cards, which are also poems, like
the typewriter writing the letter
one little tooth at a time, one love at
a time, in our city of paper and crows.

//

BROWN REFRIGERATOR

You don't have to understand it
but you will carry it anyway.
Like that couple whose baby died,
when they had to move
to another state, they took the baby
from the years-long ground
and brought her with them.
They did this again a second
time, their memory always
tied to its embodiment,
new burials for an old grief.
In a short film I once saw,
ants lifted away the silver
and gold confetti from a party,
making a trail of suns
and moons on the floor.
The filmmaker must have put
something sweet on the circles,
like a painter dabbing
little points of white paint
to give highlights to an eyeball.
Some of the recipes that
a friend keeps making
go so far back in her family
that the recipes are like snapshots
of villages and forests,
mountains and falling snow.
Apples and trout rise up
into the night's constellations,
a dark without yellow stars.
What I remember of childhood
sometimes comes down

to the brown refrigerator
in our house. Its chrome
handle was always angry
with static, so that now when
I reach for the doorknob
or the gas pump, the sharp
charge on my fingers is
childhood calling its child back.

DAGUERREOTYPES

That art should once have been marked
with this delicacy: always only one
of each thing made, so that your poem
has its one life on the sheet

you have chosen for it, or the snapshot
of the birthday party, everything
in the room upended by the children's
jubilation, survives only

in the single defended piece of glass.
One bought in a flea market
shows a woman in a black dress against
a white background, her hair greased

dark, her body's shape a Victorian,
totemic solidity. One boy
leaning on the paisley-pattern tablecloth
has his cheeks tinted pink,

his face the thumb-print oval
of a cameo. Still another: the grim old
couple side-by-side, dressed as
though for a funeral, though finally it is

triumph recorded in the mirrored
surface, the triumph of being there at all,
of being accounted for,
of someone having been ordered

to take account of who you are.
I buy them wherever I see them.

I seek them out, in fact. Which is why,
in the small Maine town where

we were driving through, my mother
and sister and I stopped at one
of the main street's antique shops, to see
what we might find there.

Only to have the woman at the counter
look up, shake her head at us deliberately,
her face its own chemical expression
in glass, so that we knew to turn

away, nothing said. We might have
thought something of it, our brown faces
in the glass of her face, but we made
nothing of it, instead moved on

to the next store, where depression
glass, cloudy silver, and ironstone plates
glowed their fluorescent elegies.
One bought in another flea market

shows a little girl and her older brother,
the girl holding a small bouquet,
the girl, brother and flowers holding
the serious calmness the photographer

would have asked for, the camera's eye
needing the long exposure's gaze
to etch them there, deep with eternity.
Still another, and this one rare

and costly, shows a farm's winter scene:
band of white sky and snow-fallen
hills in the background, frozen white lake
in the middle, and in the foreground

the snug fenced house, surrounded
by old trees. Everything a silent intricacy:
the chimney is smokeless,
the snowy lake is a glare of unwritten

paper. In the hot, green place where
I was born, I don't know if this technology
ever had its time, the elegant glass
now oxidizing in boutique cases and quiet

attics, in a place that had no attics,
and no people, apparently, worth keeping
in the expense of solvents.
The pleasure and civility of a young

man's bow-tie, a boy in a sailor cap,
the girls with thin ribbons on their necks,
the silk simple and clean as cuts.
I put my eye close to each bought surface.

ODE: 1975

What did I know that my parents didn't give me?
Even the house-shaking storm
seemed one more event of their conjuring,
our house a crystal globe in the tropical dark.

Inside, my sister and I shaped a puzzle into a new place:
a castle with turrets, white as a swan.

It wasn't a mere storm but a *typhoon*, one kind
of cognate for the wind and rain
that brought the trees' faces to our windows.

At first the cheer of my mother in the kitchen,
my father caught at home. Then the electricity gone,
the candles poised on bottles.

Childhood, a house defined, set apart.
Gold and lavender, green and black, orange and brown.

Once, my father took me to a field.

A ring of spectators brewed around two horses
that had been brought there.
A third, a mare, was in heat, neighing at the side.
It was held by a rope while the two stallions raged

for wanting her. The circumference of the crowd grew
and shrank around the fighting:

foaming teeth, hooves, brown dust raising its own storm
over the brown horses.

My father was everywhere and nowhere.

First his hand on my head, then lost among the quietly
expectant others, his white shirt indistinct,
remote as the snows of a later country.

PARTICLE AND WAVE

For example there was the afternoon
    I walked into her room

and she had been tied down
by the granddaughter meant to take care

    of her. The granddaughter,

who was my teenaged aunt,
    explained with no apology

that the woman had been at the rashes
which by now covered her

    arms and legs, resistant to
the Calamine applied to them.

I would have been five or six, she close
to ninety, bird-small and

    bird-gray, her face an eroding
gray image, eyes and bones.

This shows that memory can be particle,

    that it is a certain justice
carried in time, the shape of it

exact in mind, long after the faded
fact. For years after that,

    there seemed only waves
depositing their silt, then taking away

what they first gave: the guava tree
we made a kind of house,

the wire from a fence that pierced

        my cheek, the killed pig's acrid
screaming from someone's backyard,

things coming to mind
then pushing past the mind, memory as

        its very opposite, a sea
unmarked by particularity, by nothing.

I remember coloring a picture-book
        while my grandmother and aunts

swore to each other, not knowing
        what to do about the old, dying

woman in the other room. I didn't know

if a lesson was intended in my being
allowed to stay there, to listen,

to see. What I knew was this: when I looked
        back at my picture,

there was nothing more I could do with it.

VIRGIN OF GUADALUPE

Today the hole in my heart contains
the Virgin of Guadalupe, as though my heart

were a cabinet with another cabinet in it,
a wooden box the size of a small safe,

and the Virgin within in a white tunic,
blue cloak, a sash the pink of a pencil eraser.

Taken from house to house, the box
slowly got heavy with the money slipped

into a slot at the base. Behind glass, behind
the two latched shutters that opened

like windows to a view, the Virgin was
something that glowed and stayed in place

at the same time, like the fire in a fireplace,
her hands in prayer shaped like a flame,

eyes so black and sharp my sister and I knew
not to look there. There was the palm tree

out front, many stories high, that was also
a god. There was the manzanita tree

in the backyard, its soft berries red as holly,
also a god. Our dog had ticks the size of

ladybugs, afternoon radio dramas poured
from the green radio, the maid ironed

our clothes with a charcoal-filled iron, rusty
and reptilian. I don't remember her name,

but I remember a love so sharp that it leaves
the language I now have a puzzled guest

in my own memory, puzzled by the dog
found drowned in a ditch, puzzled by the gun

heavy in a drawer, the boxes from the States
arriving with toys and See's chocolate.

In my room I had made another altar,
the small Virgin guarded by candles, a hole

at the base of the figurine like the hole
in a flower-pot. Pasted on my walls, cut out

from the *National Geographics*, the animals
of the ark lined up for the next coming

of the ark: lions, bison, antelopes in leaping
outlines, articulations of a lost time,

like the new animals the children discovered
one afternoon, on cave walls in France.

ODE: 1986

The street went up a slight rise and then angled up
toward the left, like a raised arm. There were four utility
poles on one side: each pole was a T with wires
extending outward in a messy radiance of black lines

to the houses of the street. On a gray day, you looked up
to the wires like spines of an umbrella, on blue days
you forgot them because what you noticed were the trees,
and the blue past them. Our house was on the right,

middle of the block. In the first half of our life in it,
it was a cream-colored house with blue and red trim.
Later, we had it painted a light olive and a dark
green, the colors of river stones. In one part of the yard:

a pergola the potato vines took over, a continuous mass
of small white flowers. Lavender bushes in a row
on one side of the house, roses in a long row on one edge
of the side yard. The roses had always been there.

At the back: the apple-pear tree with black arthritic
branches, the sour tangerine tree beside it, and beside that,
the holly tree with pricking leaves. On the patio
was an old claw-foot tub converted into a flowerbed:

agapanthus, more lavender, daisies that never took hold.
Directly across the street, the house I still think of
as Paul's house, though he's been dead at least five years.
I had seen them take his body out in the middle

of the day, without ceremony, on a gurney. His daughter
and her family live there now. A few years before that,

his wife died, a heart attack while in the shower.
This would be the very first death. And before our house,

built in the 1920s, before the other houses on our street,
what stood? You could see the way down the hill
to Lake Merritt. But our house. The very house that is
like a center in the mind of the place, and my mind also.

QUESTION ARISING WHILE LISTENING TO
A LECTURE ON THE NATURE OF METAPHOR

Why does it mean
something that the girl

sitting beside me,
her hair cropped

punk-close on the
sides, long and gelled

stiff at top, her
legs in camouflage

leggings, her boots
black as crude oil,

the odor coming from
her a mixture

of incense and some
kind of bitter,

rocky herb, that
this smell is exactly

the smell of my
grandfather's sickbed

brew, the last-resort
swamp liquid

a Chinatown-alley
herbalist prescribed

for him on that
summer at the end,

the black water
of the profane

cupfuls meeting the
black waters that

were rising inside?

TACOMA LYRIC

Because I was equipped with memory,
the sugarcane fields are still burning somewhere,
the smoke boiling gold and gray.
Before this, the workers cut down the high stalks,
and then the fire, like a large animal,
was made to graze away the stubble.
How sweet everything is,
                              even though I am
on a humid city street, holding pencils
bought from the drugstore. On my block
there is an Irish bar, a lawnmower repair shop,
and an assisted-living facility. All this
seems insistently American, like a sky drunk

with fireworks. To my grandfather the fields
meant one kind of money, to the workers
they meant another. I was six years old
and royal, standing on the rusty hood of a Jeep.
At some point my grandfather lost
everything.
                   How insistent memory is,
so that even now I can still remember
the shoe store that is now a cupcake place,
the nail salon where there is now a coffee shop.
One winter killed the magnolia sapling
we planted in the yard, another killed
the hydrangea bush that was supposed to light up
with pink flowers.
                          When my grandfather
was old, he never said anything
about what we left behind. He loved gambling
and baseball. He died of cancer in 1996.

Sometimes we hear people roaring
out of the bar, and sometimes the screaming
from assisted-living makes the fire-trucks visit.
The things we look at keep changing:
one day's sun or another day's rain; early poppies
one day, late tomatoes another.

                           As though
each day was trying to say something,
with a voice that isn't coming from any throat.

CHORD

—Consorcia Alvarez Barot, 1913–2005

1. Annunciation

It is not always joy
          that is announced to you
in the ordinary light.

Not always a wing
          or a flood of new knowledge

delivering its atoms of change
to your body.
          Sometimes it is

a wound delivered,
just as plainly as in those
          paintings, her head tilted

up or down, in an angle of
          resignation and responsibility.

No fanfare in the room
other than some structure inside you
          made flat

by what you have received,
          the heart a putty-colored

folding chair knocked
to the ground.
          And the room itself, emptied,

this is part of the recognition.
      The room a wound,
       the light a wing on the floor,

the atoms of dust
      in the shaft. And the quiet,
that is grief's appetite.

2. Grasshopper

it was in the middle of the night
the middle of dying   the houses slept
but we did not sleep   it was not
dark   it was not dark

        memory not so much a plow
        not the fierce direction   into
        the layered ground   but like light's
        refraction   light breaking

we surround the hole of the
room of dying   we surround her mouth
the hole of clear air   the portal
of waiting   watching the hole

        the light breaking against bright
        surfaces   then springing on others
        on leaf and on face   on
        water   gray as a breastplate

light breaking on the oxygen tank   on the
instruments of   medical measure
and above us   the dresser's figurine
Mary   her dress pink as a mouth

        light breaking against the daughter
        taking a pulse   another praying against
        a corner   in the breath's
        duration   in the indrawn breath

why not see it simply as lost   blood
pressure   the breath ceasing
one unreleased gasp   why not see it
as body   parting with its function

        her face is   a fall leaf parchment
        I am writing   her face
        I am writing   a parchment love
        the parchment   I am writing upon

and no alarm at all   with her stopped breath
something like a cheer   going up
among us   the accomplishment
of an arrival   the cheer and wailing

        and memory now not so much catching
        as caught   in the labyrinth
        designed like a thumb's whorls
        caught   while in wonder's order

then there was the speck they
saw   in the room afterwards   the grasshopper
green live contraption   contriving grief
the grief that is   green in December

3. Threnody

Chord that is your satin purple dress, love's good synesthesia.

Chord that is your classroom's chalked board, its elementary figures.

Chord that is letters, that is photo albums, that is rosaries, that is money.

Chord that is the lion-gold hills along the Central Valley, our I-5 songs.

Chord that is your young husband, outlived longer than he lived.

Chord that is a photograph of you among tulips, the field now no field.

Chord that is time, that is children, that is houses, that is countries.

Chord that is your name, conjugation for the sun and for consolation.

Chord that is your throat, its Sunday hymns unabashed, unstricken.

INVENTORY

Bridges and streets. The neon like candy.
Brake lights blooming in rain. Rain.
Concrete. Long live the concrete of cities.

Spoon. Chair. Bed, bread, and stitch.
This language of the house. Blond
light across the mirror. Soap. Salt shaker.

The ginger of you. The cream of you.
The eyes and bones. The scratch-and-sniff
of you. The back. The back of the hand.

Crickets and prairie. The trees standing
like husbands. The gold grass moving,
the pelt of earth. The fence-posts like souls.

Lunch at midnight, dinner at breakfast,
graveyard and swing. Machine that
is the father's pet. Machine that is days.

Breath, reed. Vowels, syllables. Strings.
The bluesman saying, I don't practice,
I throw some meat into the guitar case.

Moon that is the sun of statues. Cornice
pigeons, accordion storefront gates, trash
swirled into cowlick shapes. Box sleepers.

The wish, biding inside like a hive of bees.
The crow, a knuckle of the landscape.
The stone, which is tired of the discursive.

SYNTAX

There is the man in the park
        in the middle of all that lawn, practicing
casting out, the long rod

        a curving flexible extension
of his arm, the filaments of the almost invisible
        lines making ghost lines

in the air around him, his movements
        and the craft they make
an energy I don't know how to read, other than

        to know they are a making
that must be as much in the mind
        as it is of the body, the body holding still

there in the gray of the winter
        day, winter having already
stripped the park's trees, paper birches and oaks,

        the evergreens like arrows
pointing to the wax-paper sky, the sky that is now
        visible because of the leaves

not there, the sky a white light painful to the eye
        because it is not specific,
because it is the dazzle of the abstract we are

        looking at, the dazzle of
white chrysanthemum brought back to sudden sky
        when the military plane goes

over us, practicing its cartographies above
　　　　us, the north of where
we are, the war that we are, the plane's gray line

　　　　just one syntax of thought
the day has, the way the park's
　　　　playground and its primary colors are

another, the way the homeless man
　　　　under his sullen Navajo blanket is another,
each thing a part of speech, the jogger's

　　　　purple windbreaker like a bird,
the cannon and the founders' statues
　　　　like chess pieces against the grid of the sky,

each thing forcing the eye open,
　　　　the mind arcing, like the fisherman's mind
leaning towards the shapes

　　　　his lines momentarily keep
unspooling, each line always about to reach the river
　　　　that is there and not there.

WHITMAN, 1841

I don't know if he did or did not touch the boy.
But that boy told a brother or a father or a friend,
who told someone in a tavern, or told someone

about it while the men hauled in the nets of fish
from the Sound. Or maybe it was told to someone
on the street, a group of men talking outside

the village schoolhouse, where he was the teacher.
What was whispered about him brought everyone
to church that Sunday, where the preacher roared

his name and the pews cleared out to find him.
He was twenty-one, thought of himself as an exile.
He was boarding with the boy and his family.

The boy was a boy in that schoolroom he hated.
Not finding him in the first house, they found him
in another and dragged him from under the bed

where he had been hiding. He was led outside.
And they took the tar they used for their boats,
and they broke some pillows for their feathers,

and the biography talks about those winter months
when there was not a trace of him, until the trail
of letters, articles, stories, and poems started

up again, showing he was back in the big city.
He was done with teaching. That was one part
of himself completed, though the self would never

be final, the way his one book of poems would
never stop taking everything into itself. The look
of the streets and the buildings. The look of men

and women. The names of ferry boats and trains.
The name of the village, which was Southold.
The name of the preacher, which was Smith.

EXEGESIS IN WARTIME

Hemingway has a sentence that I think of
as a masterpiece of small engineering.
Think of a paper clip: small, plain, but someone
had to think of it, actually make it. Think of
a brown paper bag: it can take just so much
weight, a couple of pounds maybe, but one ounce
more and it breaks. I'm talking about
weight and measure, the possibility for tensile
extension in a sentence, the words lined up
like the units of a train, the syntax of blue
and black cars: *In the fall the war was always
there, but we did not go to it anymore.*

           When al-Mutanabi returned to Baghdad
           in 965, he was killed by bandits just outside the city.
           In life he had wandered among Bedouins
           and princes, in the intrigues and the solitudes of exile,
           as much a courtier as a poet. Brash,
           he claimed to be a prophet. In a poem written
           in Egypt, he had a fever that came to him
           like a woman, a woman for whom he felt no desire,
           but who *spent the night in my bones.*

Two clauses, virtually two lines of iambic
pentameter, the first foot so much in
a hurry that it is missing its first breath.
In the first clause, all the assonance
blossoming from the *a* sounds, the off-rhyming
consonance of *war* and *there*, the two
words like nails holding the clause down.
And in the second clause, the assonant work of
not go to and *anymore*. The *a* sounds

in the first clause thus effect a lightening,
the *o* sounds in the latter clause effect
a heavying. The ennui and melancholy
of the sentence's content get enacted in that
rise and fall in the sounds of the syllables.

When he was off the watch, the soldier sighted
birds by his camp near the Tigris River.
He had brought that avidity with him, a birdwatcher
since twelve. Here they teemed. Bulbuls. Terns.
Squacco heron. Purple swamphen. Loud, busy,
the multitude of them at a garbage pit:
Rooks. Hooded crows. Jackdaws. Some starlings.

Fourteen monosyllabic words, two polysyllabic,
sixteen words in all. But the nub of a novel
might as well be there, a world of circumstance,
of emotional weight. In the first clause we get
groundwork: *In the fall* is time and season.
With *the war*: ostensible subject and context.
With *was always there*: tonal resignation,
something like wistfulness. The war is inescapable,
yet the tonal posture is not a terrified one.
The war might as well be a mountain one sees
outside: *always there*. The war might as well be
a lyric longing, the show of light at the horizon.

When the truck was blown up on Mutanabi Street,
it killed 30 people and exploded the old
street's book bazaar, where publishers, bookstores,
printers, and the writers' cafes had always been.
Papers with edges on fire floated down

like leaflets from an airplane. Smoke pushed into
the busted windows. Noise, and then none.

In the second clause: conflict, denouement.
With *but*: a conflict implied. With *we*: protagonists,
indefinitely ascribed. With *did not go to it anymore*:
an almost insouciant demurral. As though
the protagonists had a choice not to experience it,
the old entertainment of war now all spent,
and instead they went on with their business,
like figures in a villa, or the shocked inhabitants
of a sanatorium, stricken with a thoughtless inaction.
It's the verb *go* that's so loaded, all agency
seemingly given to the protagonists, who could,
after all, decide on refusal. And that *anymore*:
its mild, sweet, sad, beautiful melodrama.

When I read the soldier's online journal, I am
impressed by the pleasure of language: birds' names
like jewels, landscapes exalted somehow
into clarity, even when they have become a theater
of trash, sulfur, and dread. It is not the soldier's place
to explain why he is doing what he is doing.
So that when he writes of his first day, *By the time
it was light we were far into the country*,
we are meant to see the light itself, simple as it was,
and the country, varnished by that early light,
not yet made remarkable by the soldier's errand there.

ELECTION SONG

I want to be the governor of Alaska. Because the season
is turning, because the trees are becoming an announcement,
their leaves with the future already in them, the self-arson
of the scarlet leaves, the yellow leaves like superlative
lemons, I want to be the governor of Alaska. Because
I'm tired of the news, the newspapers, the public radio

experts, and my own sad inability to sit quietly in my room,
which Pascal declares is the problem with people, I want
to be the governor of Alaska. Because from the air base
and army base outside my town, airplanes as gray as whales
and as big as dreams keep flying over our houses,
shrieking like oversized skateboards on city sidewalks.

Because of arsenic in the rain, because of arsenic sleeping
inside the ground, and the weather like a cold war always
coming down from Canada and Russia, I want to be
the governor of Alaska. Because I'm always hearing speech
from the kettles and the door-knobs, those pure products
of America, their soft words always scurrying, things

bothered by eyes and light. Because I have been reading
the letters of van Gogh, the part where he says, "Instead of
painting the ordinary wall of the mean room, I paint
infinity." Because when he died the world went dark by half,
and when you went away this morning the other half went
dark, I want to be the governor of Alaska. Because of all

the Filipinos canning tuna in Alaska, because of the
mail-order brides ordered by the lonely men of Alaska,
I want to be the governor of Alaska. Because of the pipeline
on the state's chest like a bypass scar, because of the streams

and flowers of the tundra, alive so briefly they are
like the gift of an election blossoming every four years,

I want to be the governor of Alaska. Because of the price
of gas, because of the rosaries I prayed in my childhood,
I want to be the governor of Alaska. Because even then,
in childhood, I knew it was doubt that made people small,
when I was dared to eat a caterpillar, I did. It wasn't shooting
moose, but still it made me want to be the governor of Alaska.

THE MAN WITH THE CREW-CUT

This is February. The day is as good as
dead, tombed over by a month-long stretch
of overcast sky. I like reading almost as much

as I like eating. I like both better than
I like people. At the noodle shop I get all three,
where the bowl in front of me is dense

with the gist of many things. Soybean fields.
Rice paddies. Green chilis and limes.
I am reading a book on the Japanese internees

and their camps. The canine edges
of desert mountains. The planks of the walls.
The laundry on the lines gray as people.

There is always a war on, somewhere.
Someone making a sign to bring to a protest,
my aunt facing a biopsy, a city block

flattened, over and over, city by city by city.
In the book about the camps, no one talks
about their feelings. The noodle shop is warm

because of the people here. I am less
myself and more of everyone else, for a change.
Outside, there is rain. The wipers waving

valentine shapes across windshields.
That is where I am when he walks in,
the young man with only one arm, his glasses

a little foggy, his yellow hair still in a crew-cut.

COAST STARLIGHT

Out of the station. Out of the rail-yard's braiding
and unbraiding tracks. Onto the one track
skimming the edge of the coast's flat gray water.
On one side, marinas and houseboats
and the demolished timber mills' supports, sticking out
of the water like burned matchsticks.
On the other side the crumbling spread of landscape.
Woods. Little woods where there are as many trees
toppled over as there are live ones. Moss
on everything an earnest green fuzz. The ferns deeply
wet, then the junk in the poor yards behind
factories, trailers, houses. Morning, and the light is
the day's information.   ·
                              What was I talking about,
talking about the place of the political
in poems, the students writing down what I said
to them. That you have to keep distressing the canvas
of the personal. That you need to ask what is
left out for beauty's sake, to see how the unspoken
will inflect the things you have allowed yourself to say.
Now these marshy places. Grasses and cattails,
which are not caricatures of knowledge.
Pools of milky green water. And the creeks curving
into sudden sight like a heartache. The mind going
over and over things, not knowing what to do
with the world, but to turn it into something else.

TRIPTYCH

1. Bitterns

It is true, no one suspects the days
will be such gods. But like the gods, the beautiful

is always halfway to lying, halfway to what is cold.
First there is this, and then there will be

the dark. The low solstice sun is a fool's gold
on the open water, the shore's weeds have clotted

into stinking drifts, shorn like beards.
Like nerves, the flies twitch and feed on them.

The flies are like a civilization and its many desires
This is to say that even a dead thing

can be the site of another thing's hunger.
At the horizon, it is just about time to begin

the show of fire. One more god saying, *This is all
I can do with my hands*. The water has become

the color of coins. The mud catches silver
in the furrows. A boat cuts the water, like scissors

into fabric. There are all of these ways
in which the light and the dark keep being

distributed: above, the moon, divided. It is not prayer
claiming each thing in its grasp, but it is like.

To this the birds add their small, quick tracks.
As though it is ground, not fire, they are walking on.

2. Whidbey Island

On the day the artist died, not knowing
                    this would be the day,
her husband coaxed her outside and they

worked around the two tall pines that
                    leaned the same way, that stood
near each other like twins. They put

an S-curve of large rounded rocks
                    at the base of one tree, looped
the rocks in lessening size as they

rounded the other tree. A rusty length
                    of salvaged boat chain
completed the artwork, as though to say

something about how the man-made
                    was merely part of what
had always been here: the gray rocks

from the nearby beach, the driftwood
                    shaped like plowshares
and lightning, turning white among

the new rhododendrons. In the lagoon
                    in front of their house,
a foursome of hooded mergansers,

a lone heron backlit in late silver light,
                    a kingfisher hovering then
plunging, but too far to confirm if it had

caught anything. Because kingfishers
         keep in pairs, when she
found one dead from having flown into

a window, she knew the other would
         come looking, which it did.
This was not a metaphor for anything,

but simple fact. The fact of water,
         grass, trees, houses, cells, blood.
The fact of a last day's work, then

the start of dying. The fact of what one
         intends, and what happens.
The bird calling and calling and calling.

3. Lighthouse

We are two figures on an early spring beach
and what I want is to be outside
of us, to be able to read us not as we are
but as figures without story, without ending.
One man in a blue jacket and another man
in a blue sweater on a gem-blue day
and water so still that a leaf on it just stays.
The stones are so round they look
manufactured, the gulls on the driftwood are quiet
as taxidermy. I want no ending
because an ending would mean a story
I can figure out for myself, a simple story
that isn't the raveling and unraveling
of years, of thousands of miles, thousands
of words already said and not said.
How much weight is actually behind
two figures walking on the gray arc of a beach.
How much goes into a day that is weightless.
The sun is an enormous gold flower
and the light wants us to see everything.
Even down into the green bottom stones,
even to the miles-away mountains and their lace
shawls, even to the names of the ships
distant as gray cities, floating across
the sound. I want to be outside us and to see us.
The image of the side of your face. The image
of your arm pointing at the lighthouse. The image
kept like a ceramic bit of time, not something
the day cannot help but disperse.
Otherwise we have already walked as far

as we can. We have seen the yellow kayak
and the red kayak go by, semaphores for self
and self, different and the same
at the same time. Otherwise, we have already gone
back to the car. There are stones and shells in my pocket.
Dead things. Even though this is a love poem.

AFTER DARWISH

I want from love only the beginning.
Not this hillside above the twilight-awakening
city, where you are more absent
for being so present in my mind. The far
cathedral is a gold nipple, the surrounding buildings
like silver and black boxes punctured
by their lights pushing out.
                                        I want from love
only the beginning. Not the shoreline
where we spoke away the night, the ocean
an indigo sound, its edges appearing
in melting white lines, while the fog stood
away from us, out where boats swayed
like drunk holiday lights, the air weirdly still
and warm.
                I want from love only
the beginning. Not the promenade and its rain
at 3AM, the blooms of two umbrellas
and our argument beneath them, as far apart
as the two boroughs separated
by a river, so that even the stone arc
of the bridge couldn't suture the arm's length
we stood from each other.
                                        I want from love
only the beginning. The beginning of one more
conversation in a car, the beginning
of a snow that leaves the day as white
as a hospital, the beginning of an industrial dusk,
the beginning of a new rain, rain that is
the water of the Arno, the water of the Hudson,
the water of the Mississippi, the water of the Nile.

RICK BAROT has published two books of poetry with Sarabande Books:
The Darker Fall (2002), which received the Kathryn A. Morton Prize,
and *Want* (2008), which was a finalist for the Lambda Literary Award
and won the 2009 Grub Street Book Prize. He has received fellowships
from the National Endowment for the Arts, the Artist Trust of
Washington, the Civitella Ranieri Foundation, and Stanford University,
where he was a Wallace E. Stegner Fellow and a Jones Lecturer in
Poetry. His poems and essays have appeared in numerous publications,
including *Poetry, The Paris Review, The New Republic, Ploughshares, Tin
House, The Kenyon Review,* and *Virginia Quarterly Review*. He is the
poetry editor of *New England Review*. He lives in Tacoma, Washington
and teaches at Pacific Lutheran University, where he directs the Rainier
Writing Workshop, PLU's low-residency MFA in creative writing.